Original title:
The Journey to Paradise

Copyright © 2025 Creative Arts Management OÜ
All rights reserved.

Author: Christian Leclair
ISBN HARDBACK: 978-1-80581-652-2
ISBN PAPERBACK: 978-1-80581-179-4
ISBN EBOOK: 978-1-80581-652-2

A Quest for Ethereal Bliss

I packed my snacks and a floppy hat,
To chase some clouds and a friendly cat.
The map said 'left', but I turned with ease,
Found a donut shop, how could I please?

With sprinkles shining like the stars above,
I danced with joy, oh, what a shove!
The donut fairy said to watch my stride,
Or risk a trip on a sugary ride.

Wandering Through Fields of Light

Two squirrels raced with a daring cheer,
While I just tripped over my own rear.
The flowers giggled as I tumbled down,
They whispered secrets of the silly town.

A rainbow skated on a bubble's back,
With jellybeans lining the colorful track.
I skipped along with a sparkly grin,
Who knew that bliss could come from within?

Secrets Beneath the Canopy

Underneath leaves, the critters plotted,
A tea party bust where no one was spotted.
A rabbit proposed escaping the thorns,
While squirrels feasted on their popcorn morns.

The wise old owl hitched a ride on a snail,
Said, 'Life's more fun when you don't need to bail.'
I joined their feast, with some cake in tow,
Forgotting my goal, just letting it flow.

The Map of Uncharted Souls

With a crumpled map held tight in hand,
I set off to find a promised land.
But all I'd found were ducks in a row,
Quacking their secrets, the world put on show.

Their feathers fluffed like clouds in the sky,
As they jumped in puddles with a comical sigh.
I laughed so hard, my worries dismissed,
Who knew such joy came wrapped in a twist?

Sundrenched Trespasses

On a road paved with gummy bears,
A band of ants wore tiny layers.
They marched along in neon shoes,
Complaining loudly about the views.

Past jelly lakes with rubber ducks,
They danced and laughed, what silly schmucks!
With sunhats made from popcorn fluff,
They chased the breeze, oh, wasn't it tough?

Voyage Through the Edenic Undercurrents

We sailed on cereal bowls so bright,
With spoons as paddles, what a sight!
The milk was oceans, sweet and wide,
We surfed the waves with added pride.

A pirate crew of cats on deck,
Wore eyepatches, what the heck!
They searched for treasures made of cheese,
And nibbled gold with utmost ease.

Dances with the Twilight Breeze

The wind whispered jokes to the trees,
While squirrels giggled with such ease.
Moonlight costumes in garish hues,
They spun around in a wacky snooze.

Fireflies twinkled, a dance-off grand,
As shadows joined, a merry band.
They tripped on roots, then laughed so loud,
Dancing dreams beneath a shroud.

Harvest of Starlit Blessings

In fields of marshmallows, we would roam,
Collecting giggles as our home.
With lollipop sticks, we'd plant our dreams,
And welcomed joy with sticky gleams.

Balloons floated high, on clouds of cream,
While gummy worms wove their own theme.
We toasted with soda, bright and bold,
In a world where laughter never grows old.

Trails of the Wandering Heart

With shoes that squeak and toes that ache,
I tripped on a rock, oh what a mistake!
A sign said 'Paradise', arrows were bent,
Maybe next time, I'll use GPS, I meant!

Llamas in tutus joined in my parade,
They laughed and danced, oh how they swayed!
Sipped lemonade from a coconut shell,
Life's a sweet circus, can you tell?

Through the Gates of Dawn

I woke up late, what a grand surprise,
The sun was playing peekaboo with my eyes!
Rushed with a sock that was mismatched,
At dawn's early light, my fashion was patched!

A bird flew by, wearing a tiny hat,
I swore it was judging, just like my cat!
I waved at the clouds, they giggled and swirled,
Maybe my outfit will take me 'round the world?

Echoes of a Distant Haven

With a map upside down, I wandered for miles,
Chasing a squirrel who offered me smiles.
Turning in circles while humming a tune,
Spotted a picnic beneath a big moon!

Goblins were grilling, with marshmallows in tow,
I asked for a bite, they said, 'Oh no, no!'
They served me a potion that fizzed and popped,
I laughed as I danced, for I just couldn't stop!

Navigating Stardust Rivers

Riding a comet, what a silly ride,
Shooting through space with my friends by my side!
A fish in a tuxedo swam right on past,
Said, 'Take off your shoes, let's have a blast!'

Stars spilled confetti from polished cans,
I chased after wishes while losing my plans.
With giggles and sparkles lighting my way,
I danced with the cosmos, oh what a day!

Lanterns Leading to Infinity

In a forest bright, lanterns glow,
They lead the way, but where? I don't know!
Owls wear glasses, reading maps upside down,
Raccoons with hats, they dance all around.

A squirrel steals cookies, oh what a thief,
His little paws waving, causing mischief and grief.
The path is a laugh, with twists and with bends,
With giggles and snickers, who knows where it ends?

Footprints on the Sand of Time.

Footprints emerged, with jelly on toes,
The tide comes rushing, oh how it flows!
Sandcastles crumble, but laughter we keep,
While crabs wear sunglasses, making us leap.

Time flies like seagulls, squawking with cheer,
They steal our snacks, oh dear, oh dear!
We chase them in circles, our picnic a mess,
But the joy in the chaos, is truly the best!

Pathways to Eden

With paths that twist, and gardens that giggle,
Apples on trees, they start to wiggle.
A frog in a tux, serenades me with flair,
While bees in bowties give style to the air.

Each turn reveals snacks, like candy galore,
But watch for the gnomes; they're snatching more!
There's laughter in petals, a jest in the breeze,
As we skip hand in hand, feeling oh so at ease.

Whispers of Celestial Shores

Upon shores of bright shells, whispers abound,
Mermaids in flip-flops are gathered around.
They trade funny tales, of boats gone astray,
While dolphins do dances, making our day.

Stars sprinkle magic, in a shimmer of gold,
As crickets recite jokes, both silly and bold.
Underneath a moon, that winks at our play,
We laugh with the waves, as night turns to day.

Breathtaking Escapades

With a sandwich in hand, we skipped the road,
Oh, the adventures that sparked our abode!
Dancing with llamas, who knew they could groove,
In this silly pursuit, we found our move.

Up the hill, we tripped over flowers bright,
Chasing our shadows into the moonlight.
Each slip and each tumble just made us laugh,
Life's little wonders are our epitaph.

Between Bliss and Beyond

A wobbly cart led us down the lane,
With pies on our heads, we felt no pain.
We stumbled on clouds of whipped cream so high,
And giggled with joy, as we rocked in the sky.

The goats held a sign saying, 'Welcome, dear pals!'
They offered us drinks from their shimmering jugs.
With laughter as currency, we traded and played,
In the realm of pure glee, we blissfully stayed.

Landscapes of Eternal Hope

Past valleys of donuts, we trekked with a cheer,
Each step brought us closer to what we hold dear.
The rivers flowed chocolate, oh what a treat!
We splashed through the puddles, our day was complete.

With hiccups from laughter, we dodged a green frog,
Who croaked us a tune from his giggly blog.
And under the stars, our dreams took a flight,
In this realm of the funny, we danced through the night.

The Map to Infinite Wonder

A map made of candy led us on our way,
With licorice bridges and gumdrops to play.
We sailed on the sea of fizzy soda pop,
And who knew that hiccups could make you flip-flop!

Through jungles of jellybeans, wide-eyed we roamed,
Where giggling turtles found comfort in foam.
We traded some socks for a sprightly balloon,
In our wacky adventure, we hummed a sweet tune.

Embrace of the Velvet Sky

We danced beneath a piebald moon,
In slippers made of plump balloons.
With fireflies as our little guides,
We giggled at the starlit rides.

A rabbit wore a silly hat,
While squirrels skittered, rather fat.
The sky embraced our every jest,
We laughed so hard, we forgot the rest.

Pilgrimage of the Silent Hearts

Two penguins in a tie and vest,
Set out to conquer every jest.
With ice cream cones atop their heads,
They waddled forth on their cool spreads.

They tripped on fish and slipped on fate,
Still laughed at every twist of fate.
Bold journeys sprouted in their cheer,
Their hearts sang loud, though no one could hear.

Harbors of Forgotten Glories

We sailed on boats made out of cheese,
With mice as captains, blowing breeze.
The waves rolled in with sugary foam,
While crabs were knitting, making a home.

A walrus played the funky flute,
As jellyfish danced in their jelly suits.
We feasted on laughter, smooth and light,
Under the warmth of a laughing twilight.

Tides of Tranquility

A turtle painted in polka dots,
Declared that racing was all for naught.
He slowly strolled by the jelly shore,
With every wave, his spirits would soar.

The sea gulls squawked, "You're moving too slow!"
He winked and chuckled, "I'll put on a show!"
With every plop on a sandy trove,
He proved it's fine to take a slow grove.

Awakening to the Sacred Symphony

A rooster crowed a tune, quite bright,
As I tripped over my own two feet.
The sun danced in a funny way,
While coffee brewed—oh, what a treat!

I sailed a paper boat today,
On puddles formed by morning dew.
It sank, but I just laughed it off,
Such joys are in the small things too!

The trees were humming sweetly loud,
Squirrels played a game of catch.
I joined their wild and silly crowd,
A friendship that was hard to match!

As flowers waved their petals high,
I waved back with a wink and grin.
Life's an opera that we must try,
No maps needed; this will be a win!

The Elusive Tranquil Shore

I packed my bags with snacks and pies,
To find a peaceful place to chill.
But lost my way, oh what a surprise,
The map said 'here,' but it's over the hill!

I spotted dolphins doing tricks,
Hopping 'round in quite a laugh.
But wait, they turned out to be sticks,
Just floating there—a real gaffe!

A seagull swooped to steal my fries,
A comical, feathery crime!
I threw him a chip, and to my surprise,
He danced like it was a good time!

My quest for beachy bliss was fun,
With giggles and unexpected play.
If you're lost, grab a treat and run,
There's joy in getting in the way!

In Pursuit of Radiant Dreams

I chased a butterfly with flair,
It led me through the flower maze.
But tripped on roots—I flew in air!
Landed in sunflowers, quite a phase!

A gnome peeked out with a sly grin,
'Where's the party?', he called aloud.
I said, 'Right here! Come join in!'
We danced and sang, a jolly crowd!

A unicorn appeared, oh so bright,
With sparkles raining from its mane.
'Let's fly!' it said, 'Hold on tight!'
I said, 'But first, I need a snack again!'

In dreams of laughter, light as air,
Each giggle echoed far and free.
Life's a party if you dare,
Embrace the silly side with glee!

Whispers of a Sunlit Path

I packed my bags with snacks galore,
A map with doodles and jokes in store.
My sandals squeaked like a rubber duck,
With each step, I thought I'd try my luck.

The trees were chatting, branches swayed,
Telling tales of escapades they played.
A squirrel winked and stole my cheese,
As I danced around with silly ease.

Bumblebees buzzed with a jazzy swing,
Wings flapping hard, they tried to sing.
A sunbeam tickled my nose and cheek,
As I giggled loudly, my heart felt sleek.

Using a flower as my fancy hat,
I slipped on mud like a sneaky cat.
With laughter echoing far and wide,
I skipped along, my troubles aside.

Beyond the Horizon's Embrace

I climbed a hill, my spirit high,
With dreams that twinkled like the sky.
My backpack full of candy bars,
I wondered if I'd see some stars.

The clouds wore fluffy costumes bright,
As I waved hello with pure delight.
A penguin waddled, quite misplaced,
It danced around with comical grace.

I found a sign that spelled 'Cactus'
With arrows that pointed just at us.
The grass tickled in a playful tease,
As I rolled down, who needs to please?

With each twist and turn, I felt alive,
Like a disco ball with bees that strive.
Laughter echoed through winding trails,
As joy was carried by curious gales.

Steps into Eden's Grace

I stumbled on a path that shone,
Armed with snacks I called my own.
A parrot squawked, "You're on my turf!"
I traded laughs and claimed some surf.

The flowers giggled, swayed with flair,
I tried to dance; I lost my hair.
Their petals whispered sweet little pranks,
And bees joined in with buzzing thanks.

I tripped on roots, oh what a sight,
With laughter echoing, pure delight.
The squirrels joined in with little cheers,
As I embraced my funny fears.

With every step, the world grew bright,
As I found joy in silly plight.
My heart felt light, my spirit free,
In this quirky little jubilee.

Chasing Celestial Dreams

I dreamt of stars that bounce and hop,
On a trampoline with a thumpy plop.
I wore pajamas, what a sight,
Dancing with comets, oh what delight!

The moon said, "Join me for a spin!"
As I leapt high, I felt a win.
A race with asteroids, what a thrill,
I almost fell, but bopped at will.

Shooting stars played hide and seek,
They giggled soft, and gave a peek.
I flailed my arms while clouds passed by,
Laughing loudly, I touched the sky.

With joy overflowing like stardust spray,
I floated home on my goofy sway.
Each step a giggle, each laugh a dream,
Chasing skies, a cosmic team.

Footfalls Among the Celestial Stars

With each step, I trip on air,
My shoes are floating, what a scare!
I laugh and dance, I twirl around,
In cosmic jests, my joy is found.

The moon winks down, it knows my name,
The stars all giggle, it's their game.
I stumble through a cosmic door,
Who knew the heavens had a floor?

Gravity's lost, I'm feeling light,
I cartwheel past a satellite.
A comet calls, it's chasing me,
I say, 'Catch up, you're far too free!'

My friends on Earth, they shake their heads,
While I defy these mental threads.
In newfound space, I find my grin,
Who'd thought such fun would start with sin?

Garden of Infinite Possibilities

In a garden of dreams, I plant my feet,
Where gnomes trade jokes and fairies tweet.
The daisies laugh, they sway to the beat,
A picnic of wonders, oh what a treat!

The carrots wear hats, the peas take a bow,
I never knew veggies could party so loud.
With rainbows for forks and cupcakes on trees,
I feast on the sweetness, oh what a breeze!

A snail on a skateboard zooms by with glee,
While radishes join in a waltzing spree.
I'm lost in the colors that dance in the air,
Who knew such delight would grow everywhere?

As I sip from a fountain of ginger ale,
The butterflies giggle, their colors prevail.
In this merry patch, where laughter is free,
I've found the best world, come climb on with me!

Ribbons of Light and Laughter

Ribbons unfurl in a whimsical swirl,
I catch one and suddenly twirl.
The sun grins bright, it's winking at me,
Turning my day into pure jubilee!

I skip through the colors, a jolly parade,
Where rainbows of jokes and puns are laid.
A tickle from sunlight, a jig on the breeze,
This cosmic ballet is bound to please!

I stumbled upon a celestial troupe,
Where planets conjoined in a jovial loop.
They jest and they jive, with no care in sight,
As laughter surrounds in the softness of light.

So here's to the giggles beyond our concerns,
Where joy is the flame that brightly burns.
With each twinkling star, I'll shout and I'll sing,
In a realm of delight, joy's always the king!

The Ascent towards the Luminous Realm

Up the hill where giggles rose,
I counted the steps in silly prose.
Each rock I met had a pun to share,
With features so bright, as if in midair!

The path was paved with candy and jokes,
Unicorns danced, while I pranced with folks.
A jellybean cloud tickled my nose,
As I climbed higher in colorful clothes.

At the top, I found a slide made of light,
Whoosh went my giggles, oh what a sight!
The stars all clapped, they joined in the fun,
While the sun bid farewell, its day nearly done.

So here I stand, with all of my friends,
Where laughter begins and the bliss never ends.
In this luminous place where joy is supreme,
I found my delight, my wonderful dream!

Heartbeats in the Infinity of Nature

In a forest thick with chatter,
Squirrels plan a grand debate,
Which nut is best, would be the matter,
While owls just watch and wait.

A turtle's slow and steady pace,
He stops to smell a flower's plume,
But off he goes—oh, what a race,
And slips right into slimy gloom!

The breeze hums tunes of silly glee,
Birds dance like they've got two left feet,
A chipmunk joins in with glee,
As laughter echoes down the street.

Sunshine paints the world so bright,
Nature's canvas, full of cheer,
Every critter takes to flight,
On this path, there's nothing to fear!

Where Dreams Dance in Harmony

On clouds of fluff, we ride a dream,
A rabbit leads with leaps so grand,
Chasing shadows that giggle and scream,
While unicorns make castles of sand.

The moon wears shades, all bright and cool,
While stars play hopscotch in the night,
Fairies dip their toes in a pool,
And mushrooms throw a funky light.

With every twinkle, dreams uncoil,
In a whirl of color, sprightly sound,
A pig in shades on fertile soil,
Breakdances, spinning 'round and 'round.

In this land where fun takes wing,
And laughter loops like a winding thread,
Let's clap for joy—oh, what a fling,
In a world where humor's never dead!

Illumined Paths of Serenity

Roaming pathways lined with cheese,
Bouncing mice in perfect cheer,
Each step's a laugh, a gentle tease,
Moonlight tickles, sunshine steers.

A lion paints his mane in stripes,
While zebras snicker, "Look at that!"
With jokes and jests, the world's ripe,
As frogs put on a prancing hat.

The breeze carries whispers of fun,
While daisies giggle, heads held high,
Chasing butterflies while we run,
And jesters hop beneath the sky.

In harmony with all of nature,
We find our hearts in every beat,
Where joy and laughter's the greatest feature,
As silly paths lead us to greet!

Sailors of the Aurora Sea

A ship of ducks with hats so fine,
Set sail upon waves of laughter,
With quacks and jokes, the crew's divine,
They chart the course for happy ever after.

The captain winks with a wink so wide,
Maps made of crumbs and candy treats,
"Let's find the treasure," they all cried,
"Where chocolate rivers form the streets!"

Through jellyfish and gummy bears,
They navigate with squeals of glee,
Each wave a giggle, each breeze declares,
"Aye, matey, with you, life's a spree!"

At dawn, the sun paints skies of gold,
While sailors dance, their hearts so free,
As legends of their journey unfold,
On this wild, delightful sea!

Embracing the Aetherial

Through clouds I float on a marshmallow dame,
With jellybean visions and wisps of fame.
I trip on the stars, what a sight to behold,
Wearing socks with sandals, it's a journey bold.

I ride on a pencil, a quirky old steed,
With glittery rainbows, the oddest of creed.
The sun waves hello, I'm his favorite clown,
As I dance with the daisies in a polka dot gown.

Shadows of the Dawn's Promise

Awake with the roosters, my alarm clock's tease,
Coffee in hand, I'm not yet a tease.
The shadows are funny, they jiggle and prance,
While I ponder if squirrels stand a chance.

I chase after sunlight, it slips through the trees,
Wearing mismatched shoes, as light as a breeze.
Who knew that the path to the golden surprise,
Was paved with banana peels and lollypop skies?

Smiles in Misty Meadows

In meadows of giggles, the flowers all sway,
Chasing butterflies that color the day.
A bumblebee grins, with a wink and a nod,
As I skip through the grass, feeling quite odd.

With puddles reflecting my baffled delight,
I leap like a frog, what a comical sight!
The breeze chuckles softly, teasing my hair,
As I twirl with the daisies, without a care.

Ascending into the Ethereal Light

Up on a cloud that's as soft as a pie,
I munch on the dreams that float by in the sky.
With giggles I launch into fluffy white air,
Hoping to catch moonbeams, a whimsical dare.

The ether plays tricks, like a jester it beams,
As I juggle my hopes while I drift through my dreams.
In this frothy delight of absurdity's flight,
I'm just a lost soul, who forgot how to write.

Hues of the Sacred Meadow

In a field of green, I tripped and fell,
Singing to the daisies, can you hear me yell?
The butterflies laughed, oh what a sight,
As I rolled downhill in pure delight.

Chasing after rainbows with a silly grin,
The grasshoppers join me in this quirky spin.
With each leap and hop, I lose a shoe,
But what's a shoe when laughter's your cue?

The sun winks down, a bright golden tease,
While ants march by, carrying crumbs with ease.
We dance in circles, no need for a map,
With all my friends here, I take a nap.

In this sacred meadow, forever I'll roam,
With flowers and giggles, I've found my home.
So if you see me, just know I'm incredible,
Living life around me is simply unbeatable!

Echoes of Untamed Joy

A parrot squawks, 'It's time to go!'
Trusting my compass, though it's going slow.
I sail on a sock, oh what a ride,
With jellybeans trailing by my side.

The clouds are guffawing, they're tickling my feet,
As I surf on a rainbow, isn't that neat?
The moon waves hello, a cheeky old soul,
I wink back and shout, 'You've lost control!'

In a land made of giggles, I throw up confetti,
With each burst of joy, the world feels so steady.
I swing from the stars, feeling quite spry,
Until a comet quips, 'You're way too high!'

Joy echoes all around, it's a zany delight,
With laughter and raindrops, the future is bright.
So let's jump and tumble, without a care,
Just know that happiness is waiting somewhere!

Beyond the Veil of Wishes

Wishing on noodles, oh what a mistake,
But the pasta replied, 'I'm not a flake!'
With forks as our swords, we fight against fate,
Sipping on moonlight, let's party, not wait!

Our dreams ride unicycles, wobbly and free,
While gummy bears gossip 'bout sweet jubilee.
Under a jellybean sky, we laugh and we cheer,
Toasting to mischief, with lemonade near.

The fish in the pond are all wearing hats,
While frogs play the drums, 'A band of aristocrats!'
Bouncing on clouds, we see what's to be,
Beyond the veil, we sing with glee.

Every wish spins laughter, a wild freak show,
With silliness weaving its sweet gentle flow.
So beyond all the wishes, let's dance evermore,
In this land of the quirky, let's explore!

Navigate to Blissful Winds

I took to the skies on a kite made of cheese,
With mice as my co-pilots, oh what a breeze!
We dove through the clouds, laughing full blast,
Dodging popcorn storms, oh what a contrast!

Through swirling cotton candy, we twirled around,
With giggles that echoed, the best kind of sound.
A squirrel waved a flag, said, 'You're not so bad!'
I winked at the sun, feeling rather glad.

In forests of candy, we found our delight,
Where gummy worms slithered and everything's bright.
Each wind that we caught whispered secrets untold,
In this realm of the silly, life never gets old.

So let's navigate these blissful cool breezes,
With joy as our compass, and laughter that pleases.
To new heights and horizons, the fun never ends,
Just a bunch of crazy, delightful best friends!

A Symphony of Distant Shores

With seashells ringing like a bell,
I danced on sand, oh what the smell!
The fish were laughing, quite a sight,
I tripped on seaweed, what a plight.

Seagulls sang their raucous tune,
I joined in too, like a buffoon.
A crab in a tux was quite the star,
He waved his claws, we laughed bizarre.

The tide pulled in, our jokes did flow,
As waves of laughter stole the show.
Each splash a giggle, every wave a grin,
In this wild circus, we'd all jump in.

And when the sun began to set,
With sandy toes, I had no regret.
For here in the fray of ocean's cheer,
Every moment glittered, oh so dear.

Threads of a Glorious Tapestry

With needles flying, yarn in hand,
I crafted stories, all so grand.
A sweater knitted with tales of cheer,
But somehow it fit my dog, oh dear!

The colors tangled like a grand parade,
Balloons and laughter, a wild charade.
A scarf so long, it touched my toes,
I tripped and fell, honest, who knows?

Buttons I sewed that wiggled and shook,
I made a blanket big as a book.
Friends wrapped up, in stitches we rolled,
A biannual cuddle, quite epic and bold.

Through threads of humor and many a stitch,
We laughed till we cried, oh, what a glitch!
In a world that spun fabric of fun,
Our tapestry's dance had only begun.

Reveries of a Forgotten Garden

In a garden lost and hidden away,
Gnomes were gossiping, come what may.
Rabbits wore hats and brewed some tea,
While weeds danced wildly, oh so free!

A sunflower swayed, thought it was a star,
The bushes debated who traveled far.
Insects competed for dance recitals,
Made movements that'd put pros to trials.

Amid roses chirped a bird quite absurd,
Said, 'I'm the best at singing unheard!'
With laughter and petals swirling around,
We rejoiced in the joyous sound.

As twilight painted this silly array,
We plotted adventures for another day.
In this quirky garden of dreams and bliss,
We found laughter where none could dismiss.

Echoes from the Edge of Tomorrow

Tomorrow whispers, quite the tease,
With promises wrapped in a breezy freeze.
Time machines made of cardboard and tape,
Chronicles spun in wild escape.

Future folks, in wacky attire,
Chased after robots playing with fire.
Floating on clouds made of candy floss,
Who knew time trips could come at such a cost?

As echoes rang from the past I guess,
I saw my future self in a giant dress.
He winked at me while riding a snail,
Yelling, 'Catch up! You're slow as a pale!'

And in this circus of future delight,
We dined on stardust till the dawn's light.
With laughter and whimsy leading the fray,
Echoes tomorrow kept boredom at bay.

Glimmers Over the Stepping Stones

I set out with my trusty socks,
Hoping to dodge all the pesky rocks.
With every leap and each silly hop,
I land in mud—oh, what a plop!

The map is upside down today,
It tells me to wander, then leads astray.
But every wrong turn sparks a laugh,
Like that time I chased a cow for half!

Each flower points in a different way,
A colorful guide, or a game to play.
I'd rather dance with sprigs of thyme,
Than fret about losing the path every time!

With giggles echoing through the trees,
I sip from puddles like fine teas.
If the road to bliss is wild and free,
I'll take the shorter route—who even needs a key?

Beneath the Arc of Endless Skies

With clouds like marshmallows overhead,
I tripped on my laces and fell like lead.
A bird laughed out loud, teasing my plight,
As I showcased my moves like a clumsy kite!

The sun wore a hat, just like a chap,
While I tangled my feet in a world of flap.
In the shade of a tree, I feigned a rest,
But ended up snoring—what a silly guest!

Amongst the blossoms, I hummed a tune,
With a beetle as dancer, we spun by the moon.
No need for a map with a friend so bold,
Each misstep we took turned to laughter untold!

As laughter rang out from a distant hill,
I spotted a squirrel, quite the thrill!
We shared a secret, my nutty friend,
In this grand mishap, joy knows no end!

Kaleidoscope of Golden Journeys

With crayons in hand and a dream to unfold,
I painted a trail of colors so bold.
Every splatter of paint made an awkward sigh,
As a snail cut me off—a slow-moving guy!

Adventure awaits on this rainbow path,
Yet I'm busy dodging a hat from a calf!
With zigzags and swirls as I leap and twirl,
I wonder if cats have a secret world?

Frogs gave me tips on how to leap right,
While I danced with butterflies, what a sight!
With hiccup-filled laughter, I made a new friend,
In this kaleidoscope, the fun never ends!

Beneath the sun's grin, on a wobbly ride,
Every twist in the road is a joyful slide.
If life's a circus, I'll juggle and sway,
Let's cartwheel our worries and laugh all day!

Songs of the Serene Traveler

With a banjo in hand and a wink in my eye,
I serenade boulders beneath the sky.
But a frog took the stage and stole my tune,
In a froggy duet by the light of the moon!

Each footstep's a rhythm; each stumble's a beat,
While ants in a line scurry past my feet.
I'll compose a grand ballad of mishaps and fun,
As I trip on the roots—oh, isn't this run?

The path is a riddle wrapped up in a song,
Where giggles and grumbles both somehow belong.
As the trees sway and whistle their curious notes,
I'll roll like a tumbleweed, sing as I float!

When the journey feels heavy, I'll dance with the breeze,
Pour out my laughter and pluck honeyed leaves.
With each joyous step, I'll embrace every blunder,
For in the heart of the traveler, who needs to be under?

The Glimmering Path Ahead

A stepping stone, a pebble grin,
With each small hop, the fun begins.
We wander off, in silly cheer,
Chasing dreams that disappear.

Socks and sandals, oh what a sight,
We laugh as we trip, what pure delight!
The trees giggle, the clouds have jest,
We're wandering fools, but feeling blessed.

Cascade of Moonlit Reflections

Under the moon, we dance and sway,
Our shadows fight, no time to play.
Each giggle bounces off the stream,
Is this reality or a dream?

Splashing water, we turn to ice,
The fish are laughing, oh how nice!
With every jump, we float and spin,
Who knew this trip would make us grin?

Calling of the Timeless Horizons

The horizon winks, a cheeky tease,
We chase it hard, but never seize.
With map in hand, we take a wrong turn,
Lost in laughter, watch trouble churn.

A tortoise joins, it slows us down,
He tells us jokes while wearing a crown.
With every mile, our steps are light,
Who knew the path could feel so right?

Visions of Blissful Realms

Bananas peel beneath our feet,
As we skip along to a funky beat.
Clouds like candy, skies made of fluff,
Is this too much? No, just enough!

Unicorns prank, with rainbow flair,
They whisk us up into the air.
With every giggle, our spirits soar,
A blissful realm, who could ask for more?

Odyssey of Light and Dream

In a land where llamas prance,
I lost my shoe while doing a dance.
The clouds giggled, the sun threw a beam,
Chasing unicorns seemed quite a dream.

With a map made of chocolate and cream,
I sailed on a boat powered by ice cream.
Mermaids laughed as I tripped on a shell,
Swearing I'd land in a magical well.

The stars in the sky winked with delight,
As I fumbled my way through the night.
They sang me a tune, oh what a sight,
And I spun around, feeling quite light.

At last, I found a tree that could talk,
It told me to dance, gave me a shock.
So I shimmied and zigzagged, a sight so bizarre,
On this odd trek, I found my own star.

Beyond the Golden Horizon

With a spoon and a hat that was too tight,
I rode on a dragon, what a silly flight!
We bounced on clouds made of fluffy cake,
While giraffes played chess, for heaven's sake!

The road was paved with rainbow sprinkles,
And every step made the world tinkle.
A giant said, 'Welcome to my game!'
He offered free hugs, wasn't that lame?

We danced with bees in tuxedos neat,
While ants served popcorn as we took a seat.
The sun dipped low, painting all it could,
We laughed so hard, it felt like we should.

Beyond the horizon, the fun never ceased,
With a parade of joy and a colorful feast.
I found a treasure, but it was just a grin,
In this zany land, adventure's kin.

Steps towards the Sunlit Haven

I tiptoed through puddles of chocolate milk,
Hiked up hills shaped like a soft quilt of silk.
A squirrel offered me a cupcake surprise,
Complete with sprinkles that danced like the skies.

Every step echoed with giggles and glee,
As I marched with ducks who sang off-key.
A frog in a tutu joined the parade,
Together we frolicked, unafraid.

The flowers whispered secrets, both sweet and loud,
While the clouds wore their fluffiest shroud.
I stumbled upon a lion doing ballet,
He twirled and he spun, greeting the day.

At the haven, all creatures came out to play,
With laughter and joy lighting the way.
I tossed my hat in the air with flair,
In this cheerful land, fun filled the air.

Voyage Through the Heart of Bliss

On a couch made of marshmallows, I set sail,
With a chicken as captain, we followed a trail.
We navigated rivers of fizzy soda,
With pirates who spoke in a jolly old moda.

The sun wore sunglasses, chilling with ease,
While the trees played jazz with the buzzing bees.
I tripped over rainbows that giggled with glee,
And danced with the shadows, just my luck, whee!

Each wave was a laugh, each breeze a delight,
As we blasted past stars in the chill of the night.
A whale played the trumpet, what a grand show,
While mermaids all cheered, swaying to and fro.

In this radiant place where silliness thrived,
I found all my dreams and felt so alive.
With a wink and a nod, I unpacked my bliss,
In this whimsical world, I found my sweet kiss.

In Search of the Enchanted Oasis

I packed my bags with snacks and dreams,
To find a place where sunlight beams.
But every sign points to a tree,
I guess, for shade, that works for me.

With water bottles and a hat,
I stumbled on a chubby cat.
She led me to a bustling place,
Where ice cream splash was all the grace.

I asked her where the oasis lay,
She shrugged and said, 'I'll point, okay?'
Turns out she meant the nearest stand,
Where lemonade is close at hand.

So if you seek the mythical scene,
Don't take a cat who's too routine.
Just get a cup and take a sip,
My journey's bliss was just a trip!

Footprints on the Dust of Delight

Along the road, I stomped in glee,
With every step, I lost a shoe, you see.
The dust was thick, it tickled my nose,
Each sneeze sent cornflakes in a pose.

I danced with birds, they flew away,
My feathered friends just love to play.
But as I grooved to a funky beat,
I tripped on air, and down, I meet.

I left my mark, a silly trace,
It looked like I just lost a race.
But who cares if I trip and fall,
I'll just blame the dust; it's a ball!

So if you find my silly prints,
Just laugh along; don't roll your hints.
For on this trail of dust and fun,
Every footprint means I've just begun!

Lighthouses in the Golden Mist

I set off one foggy day,
To find those lights, come what may.
But all I found were rubber ducks,
I chuckled hard, the fates, they pluck.

With each step through the hazy gloom,
I stumbled on a giant broom.
I rode it like a witch in flight,
While shadows danced, what a sight!

I waved to boats of tin and trash,
With brilliant sails of silver ash.
They winked at me; I waved right back,
In this sea of giggles, not a lack.

So here's a tip if fog rolls in,
Look for the lights; let laughs begin.
And if you see a duck parade,
Join in the fun, don't be dismayed!

The Quest for Radiance

In search of light, I donned a hat,
To find a spark where joy is at.
With a map that's drawn in crayon red,
I marched ahead, my trusty stead.

I met a frog who loved to croak,
He cracked a joke, I nearly choked!
He said, 'Why search for shiny flair,
When laughter's glow is everywhere?'

We hopped along, side by side,
In search of hues and smiles wide.
He found a rainbow made of cheese,
We munched away on golden breeze.

So if you seek that radiant glow,
Bring laughter first, let good times flow.
For in the end, I found it's true,
The quest for joy starts right with you!

Reflections of a Starry Odyssey

In a rocket made of cheese,
I flew past cows with ease.
Stars winking like they know,
Shooting ducks put on a show.

Sat on Saturn's rings for laughs,
Met some aliens great at gaffs.
They offered me a drink so bright,
Turns out it was just moonlight!

Dodging comets like they're bugs,
Dancing with space-faring slugs.
A galactic game of hide and seek,
With cosmic creatures, oh so chic!

As I drift through galactic streams,
I toss in wishes, I toss in dreams.
But all I've caught is an old sock,
In this universe, it's quite the shock!

Embracing the Call of the Unfamiliar

Upon a boat made of sunbeams,
I sailed to find my silly dreams.
Fish in bow ties danced around,
While octopuses formed a band.

A seagull flew with a top hat,
Declared himself the royal diplomat.
He pooped on my treasure map,
While shouting, 'This is no time to nap!'

The waves spoke in rhymes so sweet,
As I tapped my toes to the beat.
Then a crab joined in with flair,
Juggling shells in the salty air!

By sunset's glow, I found my place,
Tickling jellyfish in the space.
With laughter echoing all around,
Unfamiliar shores, I've finally found!

Roads Wrapped in Soft Horizons

On a road of whipped cream curls,
I drove my car of dancing pearls.
Traffic jams filled with gummy bears,
And licorice guys with funny stares.

The sun was a giant disco ball,
Promising to have a grand ball.
Clouds floated by wearing hats,
While squirrels played the flutes, how about that?

A detour led me to candy land,
Where ice cream mountains proudly stand.
With chocolate rivers flowing free,
I dipped my toes and yelled with glee!

But soon the sugar rush wore thin,
As my stomach began to spin.
Time to leave this tasty fate,
And head for the exit gate!

Beneath the Timeless Canopy

Beneath the trees that giggle and sway,
I stumbled upon a giant bay.
Where raccoons gave me a witty tour,
And showed me secrets, that's for sure!

Leaves whispered jokes with rustling cheer,
While squirrels played cards, year to year.
The moon was a wink away from the pine,
I thought, 'What a funny place to dine!'

I dined on berries with a talking owl,
Who said, 'You're late for the midnight howl!'
A party of frogs jumped in with style,
Croaking tunes that made me smile!

As I waltzed with dewdrops and fireflies bright,
The stars giggled at my clumsy flight.
Beneath this canopy of gleeful spree,
I danced through the night, forever free!

With Wings of Hope Unfurled

We set sail on a cloud with flair,
Laughter echoes in fragrant air.
Floating high on dreams so bright,
Avoiding birds that poop in flight.

A map drawn in jelly on toast,
With friends as silly as a ghost.
We dodge the rain and tickle the sun,
Who knew sky socks could be so fun?

With ice cream rivers and rainbow streams,
We dance like lunatics, lost in dreams.
Oh, what a sight the world can be,
When we wear flip-flops on a bumblebee!

So here's to whims and wild delight,
With wings of hope, we're taking flight.
Turning frowns to giggles, oh so bright,
Our laughter will echo into the night.

Ascending the Spirals of Joy

We climb the stairs made of candy canes,
While juggling giggles and silly refrains.
Each step is a hop, each turn is a cheer,
Who knew that joy felt so much like beer?

The stars above are made of cheese,
We twist and twirl in the evening breeze.
I've got my friends, and we're never late,
Turning mundane into a funky fate.

Up we go, with a bubblegum bow,
The higher we fly, the funnier the show.
With laughter balloons guiding our way,
Why walk when we can cartwheel and sway?

So ascend with hope, with wobbling glee,
Life's a giggle-fest, just wait and see.
We'll spiral through clouds, sparkle and loud,
In the wildest dreams, we'll always be proud.

Where the Heart Knows No Bounds

In fields of marshmallows, love takes flight,
With hearts like balloons, we dance in delight.
Silly socks on, with mismatched glee,
Who knew freedom could taste like a tree?

From jellybean bridges to soda pop streams,
We toast to our friendship with foamy dreams.
The sky's the limit, or maybe just past,
Giggling together, adventures so vast.

When our hearts beat loud like a marching band,
We skip through the world, arm in arm, hand in hand.
With joy as our compass, we lose all strife,
Where the heart knows no bounds, we enjoy this life.

So let's giggle and roam, let silliness reign,
In a world full of smiles, there's no more pain.
For we are the dreamers with laughter around,
In this place of wonder, magic is found.

The Allure of Unseen Treasures

Under rainbows that shimmer like disco balls,
We search for treasures in glittering stalls.
X marks the spot, but who has the map?
Just dig in the sand and take a nap!

Goldfish in hats sing songs of delight,
With butterflies speeding on bikes in the night.
The allure is strong, with giggles and winks,
This world is a riddle; let's try to think!

With cookies for compass and jellybeans too,
We find our way, like lost kangaroos.
Unseen treasures hide in the corners of fun,
Chasing sunsets, we laugh till the day's done.

So join me, dear friend, on this whimsical quest,
Where the charm of our journey will always be best.
With silly delights, we shall measure our pleasure,
In this wacky world, there's joy beyond measure.

Rivers Flowing to the Heart's Horizon

In a boat made of gumballs, we rowed,
Singing songs that are best left untowed.
With fish wearing hats, we made quite a scene,
Riding waves that were fit for a queen.

A pirate made of jelly waved us hello,
As seagulls played chess in an elegant show.
We brushed past the trees that giggled with glee,
And wondered if they'd join us for tea.

Floating down currents of fizzy delight,
With conversations that stretched into the night.
The stars played tag with the moon on its ride,
While our laughter echoed far and wide.

So we paddled on with our candy seashells,
In a world filled with humor, where joy simply dwells.
And as we reached shores with marshmallow sand,
We knew our adventure was perfectly planned.

Lullabies of the Whispering Wind

The wind hummed tunes of a long-lost sock,
As it danced around rocks like a silly clock.
Whispering secrets to squirrels on the go,
While clouds dropped giggles like rain from a show.

A tuba-playing rabbit joined in the fun,
With a melody sweet as a warm cinnamon bun.
Each breeze brought a chuckle, a tickle of cheer,
As daisies all swayed, filling hearts with good gear.

We scooted on breezes, a wild, merry ride,
Chasing shadows of butterflies, side by side.
Through fields filled with laughter and daisies galore,
Where even the puddles would giggle and roar.

So let's twirl with the wind, make some noise,
For happiness blooms in the simplest joys.
As night drapes its blanket, the stars start to spin,
We'll hum lullabies of the wind with a grin.

Unraveled Threads of Serenity

In a world where socks often go astray,
We tangled our thoughts in colorful play.
With yarn made of sunshine, we wove a bright tale,
Of goats on a pogo stick, cheering without fail.

The sky wore a hat that was three sizes too big,
As rainbows replaced every old, jaded fig.
We stitched up our worries, it was quite a sight,
As penguins played hopscotch in a frosty delight.

Oh, how we chuckled, with each silly twist,
Spinning laughter and joy, we could barely resist.
With knitting needles wielded like swords in a quest,
We crafted a blanket of happiness, blessed.

So let's pluck at the strings of our whimsical heart,
And weave tales of wonder, a colorful art.
For in each unraveled thread, a giggle we'll find,
In the fabric of dreams where we're joyfully blind.

Pearls Amongst Starry Nights

Under skies where the pickles danced in delight,
We tiptoed on clouds, counting stars in the night.
With marshmallow moons that giggled with grace,
We played hopscotch on beams, in outer space.

Every pearl that we found was a joke in disguise,
Like a wink from a comet or a wink from the fries.
We floated on laughter, on sweet, puffy clouds,
Where jellybeans rapped in glittering crowds.

As constellations played charades with the sun,
We cracked up together, a consistently fun run.
In the glow of the night's ever-popping lights,
We danced with the wonders of whimsical sights.

So gather your giggles, let's sail through this dream,
For pearls are just punchlines, or so it would seem.
Amidst all the chaos, we'll make our own charts,
With happiness swirling right inside of our hearts.

Sojourn through the Fields of Gold

In a field so bright and bold,
I tripped over a pot of gold.
The leprechaun laughed in delight,
Said, "This is how I spend my night!"

I danced with daisies, feeling giddy,
The sunflowers joined, it looked quite pretty.
But bees took my hat in a terrible chase,
I chased them 'round in a frantic race!

To find my hat, oh what a quest,
The daisies laughed, I must confess.
But in the end, I found a new flair,
With bee's pollen stuck in my hair.

So here I bloom, a sight to behold,
With golden laughter and stories retold.
Next time I'll bring a bigger hat,
And maybe a net to catch that brat!

Harmonies of the Dreaming Cosmos

Stars twinkled down with a secret grin,
I asked a comet if I could win.
"You want the universe in your pocket?"
Laughing hard, it said, "Just rock it!"

Galaxies spun like a carousel,
With aliens singing, they rang a bell.
I joined their dance, what a sight to see,
But forgot I was still in my pajamas, whee!

On Saturn's rings, I took a slide,
Slipped and landed with a cosmic pride.
The aliens cheered, what a wild ride,
I left with a troupe, no need to hide!

Now I roam with a crew of stars bright,
In the cosmos where laughter delights.
Who knew the universe was so funny?
I found joy in space, isn't that sunny?

Bridges Between Worlds

I built a bridge made of jelly beans,
To cross to a land of dancing machines.
They twirled and whirled, oh what a sight,
I joined in the fun, felt so light!

A toaster told jokes, crisp and warm,
While the fridge sang songs to keep us in form.
But sprinkles flew by, in a sugary craze,
And I found myself lost in a sugary maze!

I met a donut with a glimmering glaze,
We toasted to laughter in sweet, syrupy praise.
But when I bit in, oh what a surprise,
I got a cream puff straight in my eyes!

From that day on, with sprinkles on my nose,
I laughed and danced, that's how it goes.
The bridges I crossed brought giggles galore,
In a world so sweet, who could ask for more?

Echoes of Tranquil Waters

By the lake, I tossed a stone,
It made a splash, then heard a groan.
A frog yelled, "Hey, that's not polite!"
I shrugged, and said, "But my aim is tight!"

The fish jumped up, trying to see,
If my stone was a ticket to tea.
They flipped and flopped, splashing about,
I couldn't help but laugh and shout.

The lily pads danced in the sun's glow,
With dragonflies swaying, putting on a show.
But then the wind gave a cheeky push,
And my picnic went flying—a mad whoosh!

Yet here I sit with a soggy delight,
Chasing giggles into the night.
Wet but happy, I'll raise a toast,
To wobbly picnics I love the most!

Secrets of the Serene Grove

In a grove where secrets lie,
Squirrels gossip, passing by.
One shares tales of nuts and cheese,
While birds just laugh in teasing breeze.

Beneath a tree with roots so deep,
The rabbits take a silly leap.
They dance in circles, short and stout,
While owls hoot loudly, full of doubt.

A fox in shades tries to look cool,
While deer just stare, as if a fool.
With laughter bright, the grove's a stage,
Where every critter pens a page.

And when the moon begins to rise,
The crickets serenade the skies.
Sprinkling joy, like glittered spritz,
In this grove, absurdity fits.

Gates of the Celestial Realm

At the gates where comets dance,
All the stars are in a trance.
A turkey tried to strut his stuff,
While cosmos giggled, that's enough!

Flying pigs in tutus twirl,
Snorting laughter as they swirl.
With every flap, they pass the moon,
Cracking jokes that end too soon.

The gatekeeper's a sleepy cat,
Who dreams of fish and fancy hats.
He yawns and mutters, 'Not today,'
As bright-eyed sprites just want to play.

So come and join the cosmic cheer,
Where every worry disappears.
In this realm of silly sights,
Even sadness takes flight on nights.

Chasing Starlit Reflections

In the night where shadows prance,
We chase reflections, take a chance.
A puddle whispered, 'Come and see!'
We splashed and giggled, wild and free.

The moonlight dances on our shoes,
As we spin like dizzy hues.
A cat in shades joins in the fun,
While chasing tails till day is done.

The stars above, like shiny pies,
Tease our dreams with winking eyes.
We leap and bound through cosmic fog,
Finding joy in each froggy bog.

With every splash, we laugh aloud,
Breaking through the sleepy cloud.
A silly night, with playful cheer,
Chasing dreams that feel so near.

Trails of the Everlasting Bloom

On trails where laughter colors bright,
Flowers dance in sheer delight.
A bee jives in a silly trance,
While blooms do bachata, oh what a chance!

A gopher hosts a grand parade,
With leafy hats and cool charades.
The daisies bob, the poppies sway,
As butterflies make their grand play.

A turtle strolls with swagger fine,
Claiming every bit of sunshine.
While bunnies race, oh what a sight,
Chasing their shadows in sheer delight.

Amidst the quirks of nature's scheme,
Life's tapestry weaves a dream.
With each petal, laughter blooms,
Creating joy in fragrant rooms.

Perpetual Dance of the Fireflies

In the dark, they twirl and spin,
With tiny lights, they grin and win.
Buzzing tales of summer nights,
Chasing dreams in glowing flights.

Jumpy leaps and giggly squeaks,
Whizzing by on wobbly peaks.
They share jokes that glow and blink,
Making shadows flirt and wink.

A parade of flickering glee,
Each flash a wink, come dance with me.
Beneath the stars, they twinkle mad,
Who knew bugs could be this rad?

Join the fun, don't miss the show,
Flitting fast, they steal the glow.
With every laugh, the night ignites,
In this dance of silly sights.

Fables beneath the Whispering Trees

Underneath the leafy greens,
Squirrels battle for weird beans.
Whispers from the branches sway,
Telling tales of the silly day.

Chatty birds drop feathery seeds,
While wise old owls cross their beads.
A raccoon dreams of treasure maps,
In shadows where the sunlight naps.

Each trunk holds a secret or two,
Of brave raccoons and a sneaky crew.
They build castles from twigs and leaves,
In stories that the forest weaves.

Just look closely, they dance a jig,
With every leaf, they might get big.
In this lively nook of cheer,
Lies the magic of the year.

Chronicles of the Celestial Wanderer

Stars above, a playful crew,
Comets zooming past, who knew?
Planets giggle, spin and whirl,
While moons are wrapped in laughter's twirl.

Rockets made of candy dreams,
Sailing through the cosmic beams.
With each blast, they pop and zing,
Tales of wonder they all bring.

Chasing meteors like cats,
Puppies bounce on starlit mats.
Galaxies sing a silly tune,
As they boogie past the moon.

Adventurers drift in spacesuits,
On a quest for dancing roots.
In the cosmos, fun's the rule,
Where smiles shine in every school.

Enchanted Skies above

Clouds like marshmallows float on by,
As unicorns twirl and butterflies fly.
Rainbows giggle when they arch,
Creating paths for fun to march.

The sun plays peekaboo with the stars,
As whimsical creatures drive quirky cars.
They race through the air with laughter so loud,
In the land where dreams make up the crowd.

Winds whisper jokes to every flower,
In a game of fun with every hour.
Dancing raindrops form a band,
With a beat that's goofy and grand.

Look up high, what a sight to see,
The sky's a playground, wild and free.
Join the fest in this air of bliss,
A world where none can miss the kiss.

A Tapestry of Kindred Destinations

In a bus full of clowns, we took off with glee,
Peanut butter sandwiches were our treaty.
The GPS was lost, oh what a surprise,
We ended up chasing rabbits and butterflies!

With every wrong turn, our spirits would rise,
The guide spoke in riddles, oh what a guise!
We found a big puddle, thought it was a pool,
Splashing like kids, we felt like such fools!

Each stop brought new snacks, and wild tales to share,
A llama named Larry peeked in with great flair.
We danced with the chickens, we sang with the cows,
In our quest for lost treasures—we just took our bows!

At the end of our quest, we found a soft bed,
With dreams of lost socks and jellybean spreads.
We laughed 'til we cried—it was silly but bright,
In our tapestry woven, everything felt right.

Legends Along the Winding Way

Three friends in a minivan, music cranked high,
We promised adventure beneath the blue sky.
With a map made of pizza, we set out to roam,
Each stop was a treasure, we never felt alone.

In a forest of giants, we spotted a gnome,
He offered us cookies, said, "Take 'em, they're home!"
With crumbs on our faces, we laughed till we cried,
For moments like these, we cherished the ride.

A detour through jelly, oh what a delight,
We donned sticky suits, a sugary sight!
With laughter like thunder and smiles that won't fade,
We danced through the splendor, our own grand parade.

As stars filled the heavens, we settled our heads,
Dreaming of journeys, our hearts were widespread.
And when dawn approached, with memories made,
We'd wander again, through adventures unlaid.

Serenity in the Whispering Breeze

A rickety old bicycle, we hopped on for fun,
Racing down hills, we sang like the sun.
The breeze played with hair, tickled our cheeks,
In a world full of whimsy, we felt so unique.

A sandwich attack on a picnic so grand,
With ants as our company, we took a bold stand.
We found a tall cactus and made it our friend,
Naming it Spike, and we swore it won't end!

Through fields of wild daisies, we frolicked with glee,
Trading our worries for laughter and tea.
A butterfly joined us, its wings full of shade,
We swirled in our dance, none of us afraid.

As twilight enfolded our joyous delight,
We gathered our stories, with stars shining bright.
Riding off quietly, our hearts felt at ease,
For in our small world, we found joy in the breeze.

Meadows of Imagination

We packed up our dreams in a suitcase of fun,
With crayons and markers, we each were a sun.
Through fields of imagination, we raced with delight,
Inventing wild tales that took flight in the night.

A dragon named Ziggy joined us for lunch,
His favorite treat was a peanut butter crunch.
With laughter erupting, we spoke of our fate,
In worlds full of giggles, we couldn't be late.

The hills rolled like cupcakes, all icing and cream,
Each laugh a balloon, bubbling up in a dream.
With fairies and goblins weaving tails so grand,
We skipped through the stories, hand in sticky hand.

As the sun dipped away, we settled to rest,
With pillows of clouds, we felt truly blessed.
In meadows of stories, with friends by our side,
We painted our sunsets with joy and with pride.

www.ingramcontent.com/pod-product-compliance
Lightning Source LLC
Chambersburg PA
CBHW072216070526
44585CB00015B/1359